WILDERNESS LEGEND
GRIZZLY

NorthWord Press
5900 Green Oak Drive
Minnetonka, Minnesota 55343
1-800-328-3895

Cover design by Russell S. Kuepper.
Book design by Amy J. Quamme.

National Wildlife Federation® is the nation's largest conservation, education and advocacy organization.
Since 1936, NWF has educated people from all walks of life to protect nature, wildlife and the world we
all share.

For more information about National Wildlife Federation, write: National Wildlife Federation, 8925
Leesburg Pike, Vienna, Virginia 22184.

NWF's World Wide Web Site www.nwf.org provides instant computer access to information about
National Wildlife Federation, conservation issues and ideas for getting involved in protecting our world.

©National Wildlife Federation, 1999 ™ and ® designate trademarks of National Wildlife Federation
and are used, under license, by Creative Publishing international, Inc.

Library of Congress Cataloging-in-Publication Data
Laycock, George.
    Grizzly: wilderness legend / by George Laycock ; photography
by Henry H. Holdsworth.
       p. cm. — (NorthWord wildlife series)
    Includes bibliographical references.
    ISBN 1-55971-719-X (sc)
      1. Grizzly bear. I. Holdsworth, Henry H. II. Title. III. Series.
QL737.C27L389 1997
599.784—dc21   96-37144

Printed in Malaysia

WILDERNESS LEGEND
GRIZZLY

by George Laycock
photography by Henry H. Holdsworth

Acknowledgments

Any writer telling the grizzly bear story is deeply indebted to the many predecessors whose recorded findings and observations help us better understand the great bear. But I am especially grateful to the numerous field biologists and scientists who shared with me years of experience and observations. Some of these modern bear biologists deserving special mention for their generous help are Larry Aumiller, Kerry Gunther, Stephen Herrero, Charles Jonkel, David Mattson, Michael Pelton, Dick Russell, John Schoen, Paul Schullery and Chris Servheen. Librarians and archivists were, as always, most helpful. My wife Ellen's skillful editing is reflected in these pages.

NORTHWORD®
NORTHWORD PRESS
Minnetonka, Minnesota

To wild bears everywhere
and to those who study them

Table of Contents

PREFACE

W e have long feared and hated the large predators that might attack us or dare to take the sheep, calf, or even the wild elk or deer that we wanted for ourselves. The grizzly bear, most powerful of all the wild predators, was guaranteed a special place in our folklore. Bear stories telling of blood spilled and bones broken made the grizzly larger than life and helped justify shooting, trapping and poisoning bears wherever we found them. But beyond that, we destroyed the wilderness—and with it went all its parts including the grizzly bears. Wherever the great grizzly or brown bear lives today our actions still threaten its future.

As a wild animal becomes rare, human attitudes change. In recent years people came to believe that the grizzly bear, like the bald eagle, has a special role in this world we share. For the first time we began searching for ways to rescue the grizzlies where they are vanishing and to protect them where they still prosper.

The giant bear is a complex creature. I have tried in this book to go beyond the fables, fears and folklore and find what makes the mighty grizzly bear unique among Earth's wild animals.

The most powerful predator, a grizzly's only enemies are humans.

Chapter One

IN GRIZZLY COUNTRY

W hen the grizzly bear moves through its world, other animals get out of the way. The bear has awesome power—and the independent spirit that comes with living at the very top of its food chain. There simply is no other wild animal out there, with the possible exception of another bear, eager to pick a fight with a grizzly.

We go into this giant bear's world with the uneasiness of trespassers. This is where the grizzly bear lives and we never know how it will react when we meet. Chances are the bear doesn't know either. We understand that the bear probably will not attack if we give it space, and don't provoke it. We also realize that bear stories are universally overblown and that the grizzly is less a threat than most people believe. But none of this matters because the grizzly's response to our presence is always unpredictable.

Tracks of the grizzly warn wilderness hikers
that they have entered the great bear's domain.

Just finding the broad track left by a grizzly bear can raise hairs on the back of the neck, as renowned naturalist Adolph Murie once learned. Beginning in 1922, Murie worked as a government research biologist in the wilds of Mt. McKinley National Park (now Denali) where he observed the behavior of grizzly bears and other wild animals for the next quarter-century. Years later he could still recall seeing his first grizzly bear track, a single impression where the great bear had pressed its broad padded foot down in the mud. As Murie wrote in his book, *A Naturalist In Alaska:* "You examine the landscape sharply . . . The bear is somewhere, and may be anywhere. The country has come alive."

Lance Olsen, a Montana fan of bears and one of the founders of the Great Bear Foundation says "the grizzly makes the woods wild."

This was reaffirmed for me in the half-light of an Arctic evening when a little group of us stood outside our tents sipping coffee and sharing the day's observations. *Audubon* magazine had sent us to the wild north slope of the Brooks Range within the Arctic National Wildlife Refuge to study the potential impact of the petroleum industry on this last great wilderness of the Far North.

We spoke quietly as befits intruders in the wilderness—so quietly that the large chocolate brown bear suddenly emerging from the dwarf willows bordering the creekbed three hundred yards from us did not yet realize that strangers had invaded his space. A grizzly bear commands instant attention and all of us spotted the bear immediately. Since first climbing from the small plane that ferried us north from Fairbanks, the probability of meeting a grizzly was never far from our thoughts.

New arrival or old-timer, you simply don't ignore the grizzly when you share its space. You can't overlook that combination of size and muscular structure. The great bear can run at racehorse speed, barrel tank-like through the thickest brush without slowing and kill a bull elk with a single swat of a paw. It can flip over hundred-pound rocks in search of bite-sized rodents or tear apart logs to get at hidden ants. If it chooses, the grizzly can break into cabins by simply ripping off enough siding to admit its bulk. One notorious grizzly that lived in northwestern Montana was remembered for bending a hunter's rifle barrel. Another one, with almost unbelievable strength in its jaws, bit through a cast iron skillet.

Standing erect, the grizzly checks out strange odors and sounds
before moving on—or charging.

When we came into the North Country, we hoped to see a bear, perhaps off on a distant tundra-clad mountainside. But this one, and he looked to be a large, mature animal, was too close for comfort. Besides, he was headed directly for our camp as we waited to see how the bear would react once he discovered us.

Our wait was brief. The grizzly winded us, stopped, lifted his broad head, then stood up to his full height of perhaps nine feet. Our little camp of tents and people must have been a strange and puzzling element in his quiet world. He dropped abruptly to all four feet and hit the ground running. He angled off to the east and never looked back. He was still running when he topped the ridge half a mile away and disappeared.

Sticks, Stones and Grizzlies

Long before European people arrived in the American West, the early people who came to North America from Asia must have held bears in special veneration. These hunters and gatherers, with their Stone Age weapons, did not attack the great bear casually. It is one thing to kill a grizzly with a high-powered modern rifle, another to tackle it with spears and arrows. The primitive hunter, attempting this alone, was fortunate to survive. If he were lucky enough to bag his bear, he might rise to the ranks of a respected leader in his clan and proudly wear his bear claw necklace as a badge of high honor.

More often, an attack on the grizzly was a group project in which half a dozen or more hunters joined forces and tried to bring the bear down. Time-honored ceremonials often accompanied the bear hunt. In some Native American tribes it was traditional to ask the bear's forgiveness for killing it. It is said that the Maidu people of California approached bear dens near the end of the bear's winter hibernation and called out to the bear to stand up and let them shoot it. The first hunter ran in close and shot an arrow at the sluggish grizzly, then, with the grumpy bear in pursuit, dashed off at an angle leading it toward a tree where the next shooter was hiding. When the system worked, this relay continued until the grizzly, carrying arrows like a pin cushion, fell before the exhausted, but always respectful, hunters.

The grizzly holds a special place in Native American lore and tradition.
Next pages: A fishing bear pauses to investigate a trespasser on its claim.

13

Among some people there was a taboo against eating the flesh of a grizzly bear because the bear ate people and to reciprocate would be cannibalism. But other tribes believed that eating the vital parts of a grizzly bear was a sure way to instill courage in young hunters. This "you are what you eat" thinking was reported by Chief Plenty Coups of the Crows. He recalled his grandfather bringing together young hunters and holding high above his head the dripping heart of a grizzly bear. Each boy then dutifully consumed his portion of the raw

*The abundance of fish leaves this old bear heavy with stored fat
for the coming winter.*

organ and could claim, lifelong, that he had the heart of the grizzly. Plenty Coups, years later when he lived much like the white men, would still remind himself on difficult days, "I have the heart of a grizzly bear."

Some native people, after killing a bear, paid homage to it with elaborate ceremony. Even after the bear was dead, its spirit hovered nearby, and how you treated the vanquished bear was certain to determine your future success or failure as a bear hunter. The procedure sometimes included laying out ceremonial clothes for the vanquished bear to wear into the spirit world. All this came amidst assurances to the bear's spirit that any future bears the tribe encountered would be killed with respect.

Bear Clans

This level of respect for the bear's courage, boldness and strength prompted many clans to adopt the animal as a favorite totem. The bear clan was often the most powerful group in the tribe. Ethnologists, studying tribal customs, believe that members of the bear clan assumed grizzly bear ways and tried to become like the bear. Just as the grizzly will claim a weaker animal's kill, members of the bear clan might meet incoming hunters of another clan and take whatever freshly killed game they wanted. In some cases membership in the bear clan was gained exclusively by birthright, but in others simply dreaming about a bear qualified a person for this social club. Membership implied a special bear-like fierceness in battle.

Among the Blackfeet, members of the bear clan decorated their lodges with paintings of bears on either side of the doorway. Some claimed that the bear relationship also gave them special mystical powers. Practicing their medicine, they conducted elaborate ceremonies during which the leading shaman wore the dried head of a grizzly bear and draped himself in the bear's hide while attempting to cure a sick tribesman with his own rendition of bear growls, chuffing, roaring, and dancing.

Eventually, such beliefs became legends to be passed on into modern times. For example, elders told stories of how the bear dance was performed to welcome the coming of spring. "Long ago," said the *American Anthropologist* in 1896, repeating the native peoples' version of the story, "the bear was a person. He went out alone and found a cottonwood stump . . . So he danced back and forth, originating the Bear dance." He told others in his village about his new dance and they liked it so much that it became a regular custom. But the bear said this dance was only for wintertime and this pleased the people too because in the long dark winter months they needed a party to lift their spirits. The bear said he wanted a lot of people to come to his dance and there should be much food and the celebration should last four days.

The Utes said the bear dance didn't start that way at all. Instead it began when a bear saw a husband knock his wife down because she danced before the people with a handsome young warrior. The bear took the husband outside and slapped him around awhile with his paws until the wife abuser promised to be kind to his spouse—and this is how the bear dance began—or how some women of the tribe said it did.

But the true reasoning behind the various bear dances ran much deeper. Such dances were staged to honor bears and gain their favor so the bears would not harm people during the coming hunting season. The bear, through its mystic powers, would know of the dance and not attack the people.

In California, native hunters knew that if they bragged of not fearing the great bear, its spirit would always find and kill them. The Wintu people knew that the strongest curse you could lay on an enemy was to say, "May the grizzly bear bite your father's head off."

Some people, however, including the Chemehuevis of southern California, simply adopted a "go along to get along" philosophy. They addressed any grizzly they met as "friend" and hoped the bear would react in kind.

Whatever the approach, whether it worked or not, the native people took the giant bear seriously—as people everywhere still do. There is no doubt in my mind that those ancients would have agreed with naturalist Enos Mills who called the grizzly bear, "the greatest wild animal in the world."

Salmon migrating up their spawning streams are a reliable high-energy food for Alaska's coastal bears.

Chapter Two

A WORLD
OF BEARS

Fossil records trace the history of the bear family back some five million years to a small carnivore that scientists call "Ursavus." Ursavus was apparently a furry little tree climbing beast that evolved from a dog-like ancestor in southern France. Then, about a million years ago, according to the late Björn Kurtén, renowned Finnish paleobiologist, along came Europe's now extinct cave bear that shared its world with early people. The cave bear has been gone only a few thousand years. But half a million years ago there evolved in China the prototype of the modern brown or grizzly bear. The brown or grizzly bear evolved from the same stock that was the cave bear's ancestor, which in a sense makes the extinct cave bear and the modern grizzly bear sister species.

Inland grizzlies rely primarily on vegetation for sustenance.

World climates changed. Mile-deep glaciers locked up so much of the world's water that sea levels fell, exposing a new broad belt of land connecting Asia and North America. Plants dispersed onto the land bridge and land animals followed, walking across in both directions to reach new continents. About 40,000 years ago the first wave of pioneering brown bears wandered eastward into Alaska along with other species, followed by early human hunters. This dispersal of brown-grizzly bears occurred in several waves over thousands of years up to about 13,000 years ago and the end of the Pleistocene epoch. Then these great brown-grizzlies began moving south from the Alaska area until they spread well into Mexico and eastward to the Mississippi River and probably on into the Ohio Valley.

The Biggest Bear

There was once another North American bear even larger than the grizzly. This was the giant short-faced bear (*Arctodus simus*) which became extinct some 10,000 years ago. This beast, weighing more than a ton, was about twice the size of the heaviest grizzly ever recorded in the Yellowstone area. It could have eaten today's grizzlies. The giant short-faced bear lived from Alaska south into central Mexico and eastward to Virginia. Long-legged and slender, it was apparently built for speed, leading modern scientists to speculate that it preyed on the camels and horses living here at the time.

The giant short-faced bear drifted into extinction along with its contemporaries—the camels, horses, sabertooth cats and dire wolves. Although changes in climate and extinction of its prey, or even early human hunters, may have contributed in its demise, no one is sure why this huge bear vanished.

Around the world, other bears have come and gone until today there are eight species left with several of them now edging toward early extinction. Most modern bears live in the Northern Hemisphere.

A grizzly standing on its hind legs is a most impressive animal—
and one not to be taken lightly.

Spectacled Bear

The spectacled bear (*Tremarctos ornatus*) lives in the forested mountains of Colombia, Venezuela, Ecuador, Peru and Bolivia. It has distinctive white rings forming large, costume-like spectacles around the eyes. They grow to be about six feet long and weigh 225 pounds or more.

These bears are disappearing rapidly through much of their range from hunting and habitat destruction. They are considered to be endangered.

South America's spectacled bears have been known to climb high into trees for ripened fruit.

American Black Bear

The American black bear (*Ursus americanus*) is the most numerous of all the world's bears. There may be as many as half a million of them.

They once lived over almost all of North America. Today they are found across Canada, south into Mexico and through much of the United States, including some areas they share with the grizzly.

But not all black bears are black. Some are blond or chocolate brown. Alaska's glacier bears are black bears with bluish coats and British Columbia's Kermode bear is a nearly white color phase of the black bear.

Black bear cubs of different colors are sometimes born into the same litter. Black bears grow to be five to six feet long and can weigh up to 350 pounds.

The black bear is better able to adjust to the presence of people than is the grizzly. This, plus the fact that it is carefully managed and protected as a big game animal, promises it a more secure future than that of most bears.

Asiatic Black Bear

The Asiatic black bear (*Ursus thibetanus*), about the same size as its cousin the American black bear, is at home in the forested mountains of southern Asia.

It resembles the American black bear and has a large white, crescent-shaped band across its chest, giving it its nickname "moon bear." These bears grow to be about five feet long and can weigh up to 250 pounds.

The Asiatic black bear is in serious trouble because of timbering, shooting by farmers and the capture and sale of bears to the pet trade and their parts to oriental outlets. It is considered endangered and could soon disappear throughout most of its range.

Sun Bear

The Malayan sun bear (*Helarctos malayanus*) is the smallest of the bears. It lives in the tropical rain forests of Southeast Asia. Sun bears have a patch of yellowish fur on their black chests—thus their name. The largest males weigh less than 150 pounds and are usually less than four feet long.

Their numbers are low and poachers take them to sell parts, especially gall bladders, skulls and hides, to the oriental trade. In some countries parts are served in restaurants. This, coupled with the rapid disappearance of forest lands, promises a bleak future for the little sun bear. It is considered one of the world's most endangered bears.

Asia's endangered sun bear makes a nestlike bed in a tree by bending and breaking branches.

Polar Bear

The polar bear (*Ursus maritimus*) is believed to be the most recently evolved bear. DNA studies indicate that polar bears evolved from Alaska's large coastal brown bears. Polar bears may be nearly eleven feet long and weigh up to 1,500 pounds.

The most carnivorous of all bears, polar bears depend primarily on seals for food. They catch them either by stalking the seals when they haul out on the ice, or more commonly by taking them by surprise when they surface for air at a breathing hole.

Found in five countries across the North, polar bears have increased their numbers in recent times because most hunting of them has been stopped. Oil spills, however, are a threat to them. So are pollutants including heavy metals and pesticides. The great white bear lives at the top of its arctic food chain where such materials are most concentrated.

Sloth Bear

The sloth bear (*Melursus ursinus*) is native to the forests and grasslands of India and Sri Lanka. It is named for its sluggish movement. The sloth bear has a whitish snout, a large whitish chevron on the chest and a black coat of long shaggy hair. It can grow to be five feet long and weigh over 220 pounds.

Biologists fear that due to habitat loss and illegal sale of bear parts the sloth bear's future is bleak. The government of India classifies this bear as endangered.

Giant Panda

Scientists now generally agree that the gentle bamboo-eating giant panda (*Ailuropoda melanoleuca*) belongs in the bear family. DNA analysis verifies that the giant panda split off from the bears. Adult pandas can weigh between 150 and 350 pounds and grow up to five feet long.

There are now fewer than 1,000 giant pandas living. This, coupled with the facts that they have highly specialized food habits as well as a restricted range, puts them high on the list of endangered species.

Grizzly Bear

These giants are native to much of the Northern Hemisphere, making them the world's most widely distributed of all bears. Scientists now place all of the world's brown bears in a single species (*Ursus arctos*) and, in North America, split the species into two sub-species. Most of these belong to the inland sub-species *Ursus arctos horribilis* known as grizzlies. The other North American sub-species, the giant Kodiak bear (*Ursus arctos middendorffi*), is found on only a few of Alaska's coastal islands.

Elsewhere, brown bears are still found in small populations in the mountainous regions of several European countries and eastward across northern Asia and Japan. There may be 10,000 of them on the Kamchatka Peninsula across the Bering Sea from Alaska, but here too, scientists are concerned for their future because of increasing human pressure.

In North America today the grizzlies south of Canada number perhaps only 600 to 800 animals. They are restricted primarily to pockets of wilderness centered in and around Yellowstone and Glacier national parks. In the lower 48 states, where the grizzly is now officially listed as threatened, it is now gone from more than 98 percent of the land it once roamed.

How many grizzlies once lived in North America? No one can say for sure. It is often written that there were 100,000 of them south of Canada when the earliest Europeans arrived. More cautious scientists place the prehistoric grizzly bear count at 50,000 to 100,000. But whatever the number, the grizzly bear has always been among Earth's most impressive creatures.

In Katmai National Park a small Brooks River bear fishes for lunch.
Next pages: This bear was named "Diver" because he specialized in underwater fishing.

Chapter Three

PHYSICAL ATTRIBUTES

It has been said that the farther you get a grizzly from scales and tape measures the bigger it is. But there is no need to exaggerate; the adult male grizzly, erect on its hind legs, stands eight to nine feet tall. From nose to tail he measures eight feet long and on all fours stands about three to five feet at the shoulders.

How much a grizzly weighs depends on genetics, age, sex, season and available foods. In the lower 48 states an adult male grizzly will average 400 to 600 pounds while females weigh 250 to 350 pounds. The Craighead research team weighed one monstrous male Yellowstone grizzly at 1,120 pounds. Alaska's coastal brown-grizzlies, the giants of the clan, often weigh 900 pounds and sometimes 1,200 pounds or more.

Awesome in both size and ferocity, a grizzly is never to be underestimated.
Next pages: A mother bear closely guards her cubs in the world beyond the den.

The female gains her adult weight by the time she reaches sexual maturity when four-and-a-half years old. Males continue to grow at least to age fifteen and probably as long they live and stay healthy.

People who are not familiar with the different species of bears sometimes have trouble telling young grizzlies from black bears. As the grizzly grows, however, it is easily identified. In addition to its larger bulk, the grizzly, especially when seen in profile, is recognizable by the saucerlike shape of its face and by the hump over its shoulders. The black bear's face is long and straight. The shoulder hump is the high point on the grizzly's back while the high point on the black bear is over the hind quarters. The grizzly's shoulder hump is comprised of muscles that add power to the front legs which are heavily used for digging. There is also a difference in the tracks left by black and grizzly bears. The track of the black bear's hind foot shows a wedge-shaped indentation at the arch. The grizzly's hind foot lacks this feature.

Special Hair

Most grizzly bears are dark brown, but the color can range from black to light yellow or almost white. Young bears are not necessarily the same color as their mothers, and littermates may have a variety of colors.

The grizzly's hair is one of the most effective insulators in the world of mammals. In addition to the underfur, there are long guard hairs, especially around the head and neck. It was the silver tips sometimes seen on the guard hairs that prompted early explorers to call this animal the "grizzly" bear.

The fur coat that conserves the bear's body heat in winter also traps it in summer. Bears have no sweat glands so must employ other methods of keeping cool in warm weather. They retire in midday to a day bed, often scooped out at the base of a large tree, and settle down for a siesta. The bear can hold its mouth open, let its tongue hang out and lose body heat by slobbering. Given the opportunity, it will also splash about in a mountain brook or wallow in a patch of snow.

Each spring, all the bears except the new cubs begin to shed. By autumn, they grow new coats which insulate them against the coming cold months.

Rough play and mock battles condition older cubs
for life as powerful hunters.

Claws

The grizzly's claws, five to each foot, are longer and not so sharply curved as those of the black bear. Claws on an adult grizzly are normally two to four inches long while the black bear's claws are under one and three-quarter inches long. Bear claws are not retractable. These are digging tools, but they are also versatile. They can pry up rocks, turn logs or open the body cavity of an elk or moose. Because the claws are not as curved or hooked as those of the black bear, the adult grizzly is handicapped in climbing trees, a fact that has saved a number of tree climbing people from serious injury.

While many animals, including horses, dogs and cats, walk on their toes, allowing them to run faster, bears are plantigrade animals and, like humans, walk on the whole foot.

Even at rest, the watchful bear is ready for instant action.

Teeth

A mammal's teeth offer clues to its food habits. Bears, although descended from carnivores, have adapted over the ages to an omnivorous diet and this is reflected in their teeth. Grizzly bears, like black bears, have forty-two teeth. Their large canine teeth, sharp and strong, serve for capturing and killing prey as well as in the threat display establishing dominance within the bear community.

The bear does not have cutting and slicing teeth as efficient as those of cats and other carnivores. But the bear has more highly developed molars with relatively flat crowns, which serve the bear well for grinding and crushing the vegetation on which it feeds heavily.

Old bears sometimes have teeth ground down to the gums from use or in poor condition because of decay. The bear with serious tooth problems is at a severe disadvantage and may eventually starve.

Growling and displaying of teeth intimidate weaker bears.

Digestion

Because bears are also stuck with the digestive system of their carnivorous ancestors, they lack the herbivore's special stomach that allows bacteria more opportunity to break down plant food and release proteins and carbohydrates. This inability to extract maximum energy from plants forces bears to harvest greater amounts of food if they are to accumulate enough fat to support them through the winter.

Senses

The grizzly bear's sight is not exceptional. It may have to come quite close before it can tell what it is looking at. Sometimes it stands up on its hind feet, looking and sniffing for added clues to help identify humans or other animals.

Droppings show that this grizzly bear fed heavily on cranberries.

Scientists believe that the grizzly can probably differentiate colors. Research with Great Smoky Mountains black bears at the University of Tennessee demonstrated that black bears have the ability to distinguish colors. This may help them judge the suitability of foods such as ripening berries.

What the bear lacks in vision it makes up for in its sense of smell. It smells its way through life, reading the wind and picking up clues of food or danger miles away. I once talked with a hunting guide in California who assured me that he had seen a black bear suddenly start running down the mountain and across the valley in a straight line until it arrived at the ripe carcass of a dead deer three miles away. The bear knows the common odors of the night and day where it lives, and if downwind is quick to detect the presence of carrion, garbage, elk, caribou, moose or another bear. Or people.

One observer watched from a hiding place as a large grizzly fed on spring plants along a mountainside. The ground was wet from melting snow and now and then a rock would break loose and roll down the steep slope. The bear ignored the rocks and kept on feeding peacefully. Thinking to test the bear, the naturalist purposely rolled a rock down the mountain close to the bear.

The grizzly stopped feeding, hesitated, then walked over and sniffed the stone. He quickly stood up on his hind feet, scanned the slope above him, then fell to all fours and set off running at full speed. He neither stopped nor looked back, but kept running until he was out of sight. His highly tuned sense of smell had apparently detected the faint odors of human hands on the rock, and whether recognizing this odor or not he played it safe.

Bears have acute hearing. Bear biologist Michael Pelton of the University of Tennessee's Department of Forestry, Wildlife and Fisheries, points out that the bear's ears are larger than they appear to be and describes the bear's hearing as excellent. Possibly bears even detect sounds in the ultrasonic range—sounds we do not hear. Field biologists found that very soft sounds can be detected by grizzlies two hundred yards away. The bear's hearing, however, while more acute than human hearing, is still inferior to that of the deer.

Intelligence

Bears are among the most intelligent of all wild animals. There is wide belief that only the primates outrank them. They are not all of equal intelligence any more than people are, but they learn quickly from experience and are able to remember and apply what they learn.

In 1845, respected bear hunter Colin Preston saw a giant California grizzly perform a unique hunting technique. The bear was lying on its back in clover so tall that it hid the animal. A nearby bull noticed the grass moving and approached, bellowing and challenging whatever animal hid there. As the bull approached, the bear changed its tactics and moved its paws only occasionally or just enough to keep the bull's curiosity aroused. When the bull finally lunged at the bear the grizzly grabbed him. For several minutes they engaged in a loud and terrible fight. Then the bear got in a sound swat that broke the bull's shoulder and, according to Preston, the bull fell dead.

Old Age and Death

The grizzly that escapes violent death may live twenty years or more before dying of old age. One aged male studied in northern Alaska's Brooks Range was thirty-two years old while a female in the same study had reached the age of twenty-eight. A grizzly kept in the Omaha Zoo lived to forty.

Wild bears may die of any of numerous causes or combinations of them. Some bears kill each other. Or they may simply wear out their bodies and die of old age and its accompanying loss of strength and sharp senses that once enabled them to find food. Naturalist Enos Mills tells of an old grizzly he once saw in Yellowstone National Park. He watched as it tried to rip apart a rotting log searching for ants and grubs. "I was so close that I could see his tongue as he licked to right and left. His red looking eyes stared strangely. I think that he must have been nearly blind, and also that he had nearly lost his ability to scent." Days later this bear was killed. Mills does not say how, but tells us that its teeth were gone or badly worn, claws were blunt and that it carried a host of scars from long ago fights and bullets.

Hikers should remember that thick brush may hide a grizzly bear.

On occasion a bear freezes to death in its winter den, a possibility in a year when food crops fail, temperatures are abnormally low and snowfall is below average. Starvation or disease may take them. Or the bear may die in a forest fire, be killed by a falling rock at the foot of a cliff or die in a snow slide. Now and then, porcupine quills injure or kill a bear. Old writings tell of rare and bloody fights between grizzly bears and mountain lions, but the lion is generally the loser.

These are mostly natural causes of death. Other grizzlies die because of shooting, trapping, poisoning or being stuck by a vehicle. The mighty grizzly has met only one creature that can consistently kill it—and we know who that is.

Shallow water makes a cool resting place for a battle-scarred bear.

Chapter Four

WHERE GRIZZLIES LIVE

The earliest known description of the North American grizzly written in English came from Henry Kelsey, who in 1690 at the age of twenty set off on a two-year trip into the wild Northwest. Kelsey was traveling on behalf of the Hudson's Bay Company which was seeking new sources of fur to ship back to England. After encountering a number of grizzlies, he wrote of this bear, "He is man's food & he makes food of man."

Little more was learned about grizzlies until Meriwether Lewis and William Clark began meeting the bear on their historic journey westward more than a century later. As they pushed deeper into the wilderness in 1805, they found a pristine world filled with surprises. The astounding buffalo herds, the richness of deer, elk and antelope,

Grizzly habitat is diverse and vast.

the uncounted millions of prairie chickens and waterfowl were all welcome sights. Then there was this giant bear which none of these wilderness travelers had ever seen before and few if any had even heard of. First, they found its tracks and marveled at the size. Then, beyond the Mandan villages upstream from Bismarck, North Dakota, they began to see the beast that made the tracks. To them, it looked grizzled or "white," and in temperament it was nothing at all like the smaller black bears they had killed back home in the eastern forests.

The Indians warned them about these giant bears and the hazards of close contact with them but this did not dissuade them from attacking the bear at every opportunity. Clark, writing in his journal about an early encounter with grizzlies said, "Captain Lewis, who was on shore with one hunter, met about eight o'clock two white bears. Of the strength and ferocity of this animal the Indians had given us dreadful accounts. They never attack him but in parties of six or eight persons and even then are often defeated with the loss of one or more of their party . . . He rather attacks than avoids a man."

But weren't they equipped with rifles instead of the native's primitive weapons made of stone and wood? Lewis and the other hunter both fired and each injured his bear. One bear fled but the second one turned on Lewis and charged. Its injury slowed it down enough that Lewis had time, while running full speed, to reload his muzzle loader and get in another shot. The other hunter added a third shot and finally the bear fell dead.

Clark's journal entry says this bear was a young male weighing about 300 pounds, then gives his description of that bear. "The legs," he wrote, "are somewhat longer than those of the black bear and the talons and tusks are much larger and longer. Add to which, it is a more furious animal, and very remarkable for the wounds which it will bear without dying."

Such accounts make grizzly bears sound more inclined to attack than they might really be. The Lewis and Clark party attacked grizzlies wherever they met them. The bears were only counter-attacking. Had those early hunters left the bears unmolested chances seem excellent that the bears would have left them alone as well.

Elk are a natural and important food source for grizzly bears.

Naming the Grizzly

A decade after Lewis and Clark returned from their journey, naturalist George Ord assigned the grizzly its scientific name. Ord didn't know the bear from firsthand experience. Instead he relied heavily on descriptions brought back by Lewis and Clark, and based on their reports Ord decided that this was truly a horrible beast. He felt thoroughly justified in assigning the grizzly its new scientific name, *Ursus horribilis*—the horrible bear. To this day, scientists world-wide know this subspecies of the brown bear as *Ursus arctos horribilis*.

Did George Ord hang a misnomer on the grizzly bear? Is *Ursus arctos horribilis* really that horrible? Ord believed that grizzlies hunted people because they liked to eat them. Wrote Ord, "He is the enemy of man and literally thirsts for human blood." This implied that the grizzly bear lives in a state of constant rage and that unprovoked attacks by it are the norm. But experience and reason temper these visions of blood and death. There is no question that a grizzly is a dangerous animal to be avoided or that it has injured and killed people and will do so again. But George Ord went overboard; the grizzly bear does not thirst for human blood so much as it hungers for privacy.

The next to meet these great bears of the American West were the famed mountain men who explored every western valley in pursuit of beaver pelts. These wilderness trappers told bear stories around a thousand campfires, and with the retelling the grizzly bear's reputation grew. Half of the fun was in the chase and half in telling about it.

Wilderness Bears

Those first years of exploration marked the beginning of North America's long war between grizzlies and the white explorers and settlers of America's West. It was from its beginning a contest the bear could not win.

In the lower 48 states the great bear was gone from Texas by 1890, North Dakota by 1897, California by 1922, Utah a year later, Oregon by 1931, New Mexico in 1933 and Arizona by 1935. Today it hangs on in isolated fragments of its original range in four states: Montana, Wyoming, Idaho and Washington. Within these states the

Grizzlies have been the inspiration for many a wilderness legend.

U.S. Fish and Wildlife Service identifies six distinct ecosystems where grizzlies live or where they might be restored. These bits of bear country are remnants of wilderness and they are all separated by human developments. Such fragmentation of the landscape isolates the grizzlies as surely as if they lived on islands. Only two of the ecosystems still have sizable numbers of the big bears.

The most secure grizzly population in the lower 48 states occupies what the U.S. Fish and Wildlife Service and the Grizzly Bear Recovery Team identify as the Northern Continental Divide Ecosystem. This area includes Glacier National Park and adjoining wilderness in national forests, Indian reservations, and U.S. Bureau of Land Management holdings. This is some of the wildest land left on the continent and an estimated 400 or so grizzlies live here where they are free to wander into Canada and back.

The other prominent grizzly bear ecosystem south of Canada includes Yellowstone National Park and surrounding country. These are the bears we know best—for this is where the grizzly has been studied in greater detail than anywhere else in the world.

The Greater Yellowstone Ecosystem, the southernmost home of any substantial number of grizzlies, encompasses mountain country as beautiful as any on the continent. Here the bears roam Yellowstone and Grand Teton National Parks and the John D. Rockefeller, Jr. National Memorial Parkway that links them, as well as surrounding national forest and Bureau of Land Management holdings. This ecosystem lies within three states: Wyoming, Montana and Idaho. These Yellowstone grizzlies, numbering perhaps 250, are isolated 240 miles from the next nearest grizzly bear population in the Selway-Bitterroot Ecosystem.

There is some speculation that a few grizzlies still hide out in the rugged San Juan Mountains of southwestern Colorado. In 1967 a government trapper reported seeing a female and two grizzly cubs far up in the mountains. Then, in 1979, while on an archery hunting trip for elk in that region, a guide was severely mauled by a large bear that he finally killed. His bear turned out to be a sixteen-year-old female grizzly. Whether or not he took the very last free-roaming grizzly in Colorado remains unanswered.

The grizzly struggles to maintain a foothold in its ever-diminishing habitat.
Next pages: Wilderness, where the grizzly thrives, is shrinking as people move in with roads, homes and machinery.

Alaska's Bears

The last real stronghold in North America where today's brown/ grizzly bear is reasonably secure is Alaska and parts of Western Canada. Alaska's bear biologists estimate the total number of brown-grizzlies in their state at 30,000 to 40,000. Except for some of its islands, these bears still occupy almost every section of Alaska, and their status has not changed greatly in modern times—at least not yet.

One June evening some years ago I accompanied Alaska bear biologist John Schoen on a flight to observe what must be the world's greatest concentration of grizzlies. We flew out of Juneau toward the 96-mile-long Admiralty Island which lies within the Tongass National Forest. Here, I would surely see a bear—at least one—because Admiralty has about one grizzly per square mile, making this island one of the world's most productive of all places for grizzlies.

Below us was an amazing system of bear trails etched into the slopes. We saw enough bears that somewhere I lost count. It is not unusual to see forty or fifty bears on such a flight.

We landed in a meadow of light green grasses and sedges. We climbed quietly from the plane, checked the wind direction, and made our way a short distance to a fringe of trees. From there we could look out across a broad field of sedges without being seen by the bears. A female and her three cubs were grazing on sedges. Then while we watched, another large bear approached their feeding area. He could not see them until quite close, but when he did discover them he simply turned away and avoided conflict.

Alaska, not Yellowstone or Glacier national parks, offers people their best remaining opportunity to see a genuine wild ranging grizzly. Most tourists visiting Alaska make Denali National Park a major desti-nation, and a prime reason for going to that spectacular park is that grizzly bears live and thrive there. Furthermore, on most days people can see the bears roaming wild and free on the open tundra and sometimes crossing the gravel road in front of the tour buses.

Whether Alaska's bears fare well in the future, or follow their southern cousins into the twilight, depends on how serious we have become about preserving their wilderness habitat. There are develop-ment pressures threatening the wild places. In parts of southeastern Alaska the government-subsidized timber industry, operating on pub-lic lands and tribal holdings, is destroying large blocks of old-growth forest by clear-cutting and sending mud down the slopes to choke the salmon streams. Meanwhile, the petroleum industry threatens the Arctic National Wildlife Refuge, and biologists see oil production there as almost surely reducing the population of grizzlies along with their neighbors the caribou, snow geese and wolves.

Canada's Bears

In western Canada, the grizzly is still found from the Pacific Coast of British Columbia to the prairie lands in Alberta, and in the northern territories to the Arctic Ocean. Although bear numbers have declined over much of their Canadian range, the country still has an estimated 25,000 grizzly bears. About half of these are in British Columbia where biologists are concerned about the impact of the heavy clear-cutting by the timber industry. Some 4,000 to 5,000 bears live in the Northwest Territory and 6,000 to 7,000 in the Yukon Territory.

There are ten national parks in Canada's grizzly bear country and they include some of North America's most rugged and scenic lands. But many of these parks are too small to provide much room for the far-ranging bears and only about 3 to 4 percent of Canada's grizzlies live in these national parks. Beyond the park boundaries they are subject to not just the stress that comes from crowding by people, but also to the direct threats from ranchers, hunters and poachers.

Next pages: A female grizzly and her young cub scan the horizon in Denali National Park.

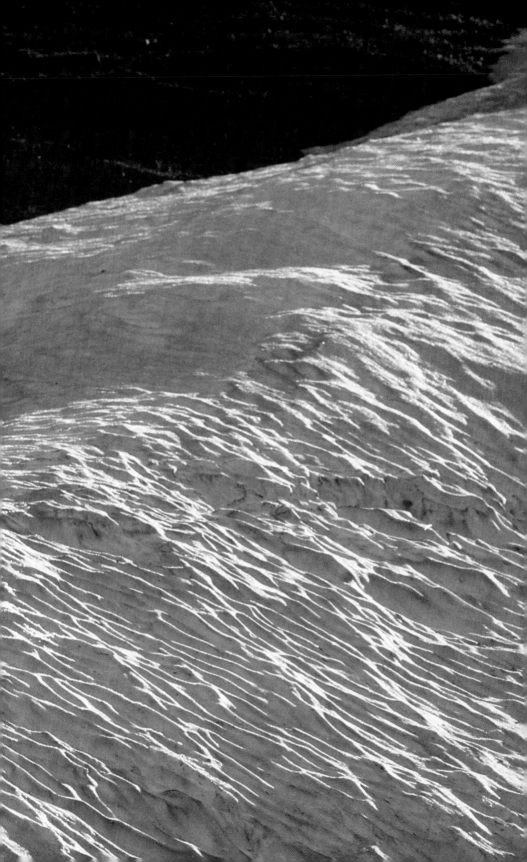

Chapter Five

SUMMER
DAYS

Late in the winter, in the darkness of his den, the male grizzly
bear grows restless, frequently adjusts the position of his body
and gradually shakes off the lethargy that bound him to the earth
through the long cold months. Eventually, released from the grip of
hibernation, he crawls sluggishly toward the gray light. He sniffs the
chilled alpine air. He looks down the mountainside and sees or smells
no threat to himself or his space. He hears nothing but the wind and
the raven. He may crawl back into his bed and slumber again. Or he
may wander off aimlessly along the slope.

Elsewhere, perhaps a couple of weeks later, the female with
which he mated the previous summer is also awakening from her
long sleep. When she emerges from her den into the familiar alpine
setting, her new cubs begin their first summer in the outdoor world.

A mouse is acceptable prey for a hungry bear.

Hereafter their years will be divided into two seasons—summer and winter. Summer for the bears is the beginning of a new time of eating, growing, breeding and traveling. The search for food becomes so vital to the bear's success, and such a demand on its time, that to study its foods is to learn much of the grizzly's behavior.

One might expect the bears emerging from their dens after months without food to be ravenous, but in truth they wander off as if breakfast is no urgent matter. After their long fast their systems need time to adjust. Their appetites return gradually over the following days until the pursuit of food becomes the principal concern that all grizzlies share through the coming months.

Since bears are omnivores, almost everything edible is acceptable. They share insects with the birds, rodents with the fox, roots with the mouse, grass with the elk, fish with the eagle and carrion with the vulture. They may feed day and night depending on the season and the fat content and abundance of foods.

Many bears, newly emerged from their dens, head first for the wet lowlands and the meadows where the tender new sedges, grasses and succulent horsetail grow. They feed on animal matter when available, but vegetation, especially grass, is always a major part of the diet.

Meanwhile, where there are forests, females with cubs tear apart rotting logs, seeking ants and other insects that supply protein needed for milk production. Where available, carrion, nutritious and easily digested, is a choice food for bears. Yellowstone grizzlies help clean up the carcasses of elk that didn't make it through the severe winter. Elsewhere too, bears eat the remains of wild sheep, moose and deer, follow the odors to gut piles left from the hunter's kill and search out the rancher's dead livestock.

In late summer, bears must begin to lay on fat for the coming winter, sometimes spending up to twenty hours a day eating. One Alaska grizzly was watched while she fed on blueberries for fourteen hours with only a half-hour off for a midday rest.

*Mother bears guard their cubs against adult male
bears that would kill them.*

Bears at Play

There are times when grizzlies pause in their more serious summer pursuits of food to engage in play. Frisky cubs wrestle, climb and roll about in carefree fashion or try to catch a passing butterfly. But even the adult grizzly, for all its no-nonsense manner, sometimes plays. Biologists have called play a "behavioral measure of well-being." Bears at play may roll, slide, chase birds, or toss about sticks and stones as toys. Adult grizzlies have been seen sliding and rolling down snow-covered slopes, then climbing back up the hill and sliding down again apparently with nothing to gain except feeling good. One observer saw a grizzly stand up and ski down a snow field on his hind feet. A bear will sometimes run at random through a grassy field, snapping in futility at grasshoppers it flushes.

*Baby grizzlies soon graduate from fun and games
to rough-and-tumble sparring matches.*

Range

Play time aside, the overwhelming demand to lay on fat for winter keeps the bears moving, sniffing the air and hunting edibles. They learn quickly to take advantage of new foods. Years ago, when explosives were planted early in the season to bring down snow slides that later might endanger trains negotiating Rogers Pass from Alberta into British Columbia, maintenance crews reported that grizzly bears found the sticks of dynamite and ate them. More recently, along the Middle Fork of the Flathead River in northern Montana, grain that spilled from wrecked trains attracted so many bears that trains hit and killed seven of them on the tracks perhaps, at least in part, due to the fact that fermented grain made the bears tipsy and so relaxed that they were too slow moving out of the path of oncoming engines.

The occasional caribou helps fatten northern grizzlies.

Within their home ranges hungry bears go where memories and odors lead them with only the barest elements of a travel plan.

How widely they travel may depend on denning areas, sex, season, social status and pressure from people or other bears. But the everlasting demand for food becomes their most compelling reason for travel. Studies in Alaska revealed that in the Arctic, where growing seasons are brief and food production limited, grizzlies may range over some 237 square miles. Those living in southeastern Alaska might have a home range of only ten or fifteen square miles. Mature males travel the greatest distances. The male may range across eight or ten miles in a day and his home range may be three times as large as that of the female.

Bears are good swimmers and even the smallest
cubs take readily to water.

One reason that females with cubs have more restricted home ranges lies in the fact that those little bears can't travel as well as big bears. Besides, the female may feel more secure keeping her cubs in the area she knows best. As the cubs come into their second year, the females cover more ground. Christopher Servheen is the grizzly bear Recovery Coordinator with the U.S. Fish and Wildlife Service. In one study of the grizzlies of the Mission Mountains in Montana he found that the bears with the smallest home ranges were young adult females recently turned out to fend for themselves. Newly weaned males also have smaller home ranges than they will have as they grow older. Grizzly bear home ranges overlap and bears do not defend territorial boundaries.

The Berry Eaters

Sugar is an important source of energy for bears that can find fruit. Grizzlies in northwestern Montana are known to feed heavily on huckleberries, buffalo berries and mountain ash. In Alaska, Adolph Murie recorded that the grizzlies relished blueberries, buffalo berries and cranberries. He wrote that the bears " . . . grazed with great vigor. Berries, leaves and twigs are all gobbled up together. The bears have too much eating to do to be finicky and selective in their berry eating."

Grizzlies not only harvest fruits but also plant them. In *International Bear News*, research ecologist Mary F. Willson writes: "In Southeast Alaska, as well as elsewhere, bears are known to eat vast quantities of fruits and disperse untold millions of seeds. This makes them vital to their ecosystems. We therefore need to think about bears as more than big tourist attractions, big game, and big threats—they are active participants in a functioning forest."

Grizzlies may also improve their habitat when they dig for roots. Researchers believe that grizzly bears digging glacier lily roots in Glacier National Park, for example, may be unintentionally improving their own food supply as they harvest the nutritious tubers. Studies show that there is more nitrogen available to plants where bears have dug than where they have not worked. In these "bear gardens" lilies revegetating the area grow faster and are probably more nutritious. Scientists see this as evidence that bears play an important role in helping to keep the whole alpine ecosystem healthy.

The roots chosen by bears are often the highly nutritious ones, so much so, that long ago native people searching for edible roots followed the bears to their favorite feeding areas.

Red Squirrels and Robbery

An important autumn food for Rocky Mountain grizzly bears is the whitebark pine nut, and the larcenous bear has found a way to maximize its pine nut harvest. The grizzly simply searches out and steals the seeds that red squirrels have cached. When squirrels begin their annual harvest in August they bury the pine nuts, but later in the year may leave them out on the ground. In either case, the bears smell them out easily enough. The pine nuts are not only highly digestible, but are also rich in fats and proteins.

Prey—Large and Small

These giant bears take living prey when they can, but they are not uniformly skilled in hunting and killing. Flying hooves, antlers and horns make this a risky business, but the bear has strength, agility and intelligence in its favor. Although bears may have minimum impact on the populations of prey animals, these losses are sometimes used to justify killing bears to spare the deer, moose and caribou in the region.

In spring, grizzlies catch the calves of bison, elk, and moose. This spring hunting for calves goes on day and night in both the forest and open fields. A grizzly good at this business may kill more elk calves than it can eat. Later in the summer when the moose and elk are so swept up in the fever of the rut that they become unwary, the grizzly can sometimes take the largest adults by surprise. The old, weak and diseased are always at risk. The bear eats what it can from its kill and covers the leftovers with brush to hide the meat for a later meal.

Those bears best able to bring down adult elk, caribou, moose and bison are the large males. The chase becomes easier if the prey animal can be surprised while crossing a stream or trying to run through deep snow. One male grizzly in Yellowstone National Park

learned to hide beside an active elk trail and ambush its victims, a plan that worked so well that he killed eight cow elk in two months. In such an attack the bear can leap upon the rear quarters of the surprised victim and simply hang on until its weight drags the animal down. Yellowstone National Park, where large predators including mountain lions and wolves were killed off, has so many elk today that the loss of elk to grizzlies is no threat to the herd.

U.S. Park Service biologist Glen F. Cole, long-time observer of Yellowstone's wildlife, witnessed elk kills by bears on various occasions. In one instance Cole watched a pair of two-year-old grizzlies chase a herd of twelve elk. They ran in circles for fifteen minutes, the bears, traveling at an easy lope, sometimes shortening the distance by dashing across the circle. Once they selected their victim, they dragged the elk to the ground and killed it instantly by biting its neck

This unprotected moose calf is easy prey for the grizzly.

and shaking it violently. They then rolled the elk over, and using those long claws, opened the abdominal cavity to begin eating.

The mighty grizzly will also claim the wolf's kill. Shortly after wolves were reintroduced in Yellowstone National Park they brought down a bison only to have it appropriated by a large grizzly. There is little that the wolves can do except stay in the area and take advantage of the scraps.

One day in Denali National Park, my wife and I came upon a photographer lying flat out beside the road. He was pointing a long lens toward a river bed far below. With binoculars, we could watch the big grizzly, guarding the carcass of a caribou on a small island in the braided channel. The photographer said the bear had been there for five days.

As we watched, a smaller grizzly emerged from the brushy thicket beside the river. She waded the shallow stream and, splashing along behind her, came a line of three small, dark cubs of the year. They waded into the shallow water until she turned back toward them. At that distance, we could not hear her, but the little bears obviously did for they wheeled about and scampered back into the brush.

As the female trotted on toward the dead caribou, the larger bear, which we presumed to be an old male, made a single bluff charge. But the female, instead of backing off, charged him with such fury that he retreated twenty feet or so and stood there, head down, watching while she ate from the caribou.

But she did not tarry. Apparently nervous about the safety of her young ones, she soon left the kill and returned to the brush. The male quickly stretched out flat on top of his trophy like a thick brown rug, and settled in for a nap.

Off to one side, perhaps forty feet away and wisely keeping its distance the full time, was a gray wolf. When we left, the wolf was still there, moving about restlessly, while the old bear continued its nap atop what remained of the kill.

Another favorite grizzly food in Denali, and elsewhere across the North, is the Arctic ground squirrel. These tawny one- to two-pound squirrels are abundant on the tundra where they dash about, nervously barking danger signals to each other. If the bear surprises a squirrel in the open, it gives chase and the squirrel dashes for its burrow.

But even if it escapes, the squirrel is not yet safe because the bear can dig it out. Those long claws loosen the dirt, then the front feet, working alternately, throw the dirt back in a shower until the bear's head begins to disappear underground. The grizzly pauses frequently and looks around. If the squirrel dares bolt from another exit, the bear rushes it, changing directions with startling speed and agility, until the

A female grizzly teaches her cubs to dig for ground squirrels.

71

squirrel either escapes or is caught and consumed on the spot. Even mice do not escape the great bear's notice. The hungry grizzly may sniff out the underground home where the mouse has stashed roots for the winter, dig them out and eat both mouse and roots.

The Littlest Prey

Under some conditions ants and other insects are relished by the grizzly. In the 1930s, hikers and naturalists venturing into remote parts of Glacier National Park in late summer began reporting grizzly bears on Mt. Cleveland and elsewhere at elevations above 10,000 feet. Nobody could say why the bears were climbing to these high rocky slopes and digging in what seemed to be nearly barren rock piles. Eventually biologists, following radio equipped grizzlies in Yellowstone National Park, learned that the bears were traveling into the high country to feed on small moths.

This insect, the army cutworm moth, migrates from the plains where their larvae eat wheat, oats, alfalfa and other cultivated crops. After flying several hundred miles, the adult moths reach the high country where they feed by night on the nectar of alpine flowers. By day they hide by the millions among the rocks on the slopes. Their soft bodies, rich in fat, help condition the grizzlies for the approaching winter. Researchers in Glacier National Park found that in mid-August, the peak time for the moth-eating bears, these moths were 18 percent protein and 35.4 percent fat.

Also present and feeding on the moths were ravens, Clark's nutcrackers and gray-crowned rosy finches. There is some speculation that the bears see the birds heading for the high country and this tells them that the time has come to climb the mountain and eat moths.

The Fishing Bears

Bears whose range includes trout and salmon spawning streams learn from their mothers where and how to catch fish. Where spawning salmon concentrate in shallow waters and around waterfalls, the bears are drawn into the area in unusual concentrations. The world's largest assemblages of brown or grizzly bears occur during the

spawning season on various Alaska streams.

Most famous of all is the McNeil River some 250 air miles south-west of Anchorage. Bears first begin arriving out of the surrounding wilderness in June to take the red salmon from a nearby creek. In the following weeks the bears concentrate at McNeil Falls as thousands of chum salmon swim upstream toward their spawning waters. On one day in 1985, ninety brown bears were counted here.

Although such crowding is unusual for the anti-social brown or grizzly bears, they adjust somewhat to the stress to take advantage of the opportunity to gather energy-rich food with minimum effort. Still, some bears, especially immature ones and some females with young, avoid these popular fishing waters with their crowds of bears.

Young bears get fishing lessons from their mother.
Next pages: Salmon migrate upstream into the jaws of waiting bears.

Where food sources do bring the bears together, theirs is not a society of equals. Dominant bears demand their pick of the best fishing spots while weaker bears keep their distance.

Bears employ body language to send warnings to each other. These signals include eye contact or averting it, walking with stiff front legs, jaw popping, mouth position, and position of the head as well as growling, chuffing and roaring. Bears fight each other largely with their mouths, and sometimes the bear's mouth is severely injured or a jaw is broken. Old bears, especially males, normally carry numerous battle scars. The encounter may begin with a challenger walking stiff-legged toward the other bear. The challenged bear can lower and turn its head aside as it submits and backs away. Or it can refuse to retreat and the fight is on. The confident victor may simply turn its back and walk away.

Concentrations of bears were certain to attract the attention of people. Each summer a limited number of visitors, chosen by lottery, travel to the McNeil River to see grizzlies at close range.

But after more than two decades of protecting the McNeil River area as a sanctuary, the use of the area by fishing bears doubled without one injury to a human by a bear. Neither has there been a threatening bear that had to be killed or moved from the area.

McNeil River's human visitors follow strict rules on where they can go, walk or camp and how they must act around the bears. As long as people around them are calm, speak quietly and do not move suddenly or erratically, the bears largely ignore them.

Bear watchers along spawning streams soon notice that not all fishing bears are equally skilled. Furthermore, fishing techniques vary from bear to bear. One system often adopted by the large dominant grizzly is to ambush fish by standing in the shallow waters below the falls with front legs spread and grab the salmon as it brushes against his legs. Others wade out above the falls and stand on the very edge to catch fish that literally leap into their open mouths.

In the heart of Yellowstone National Park lies the sprawling 84,260-acre Yellowstone Lake with a maximum depth of 351 feet. The big lake is home to its own subspecies of cutthroat trout found nowhere else. During the spawning season these trout leave the lake to swim up some sixty tributary streams where bears, as well as ospreys and white pelicans, have long relied on the spawning fish as a seasonal food source.

In 1994 a tourist caught 17-inch lake trout in Yellowstone Lake, spelling bad news for Yellowstone wildlife. Lake trout, non-natives in Yellowstone Lake, had been smuggled into the big lake by an outlaw who thought his do-it-yourself fish management would improve fishing. Lake trout, however, spawn in deep water and not shallow feeder streams. Furthermore, scientists now expect that the voracious lake trout, which often reach weights of twenty pounds and sometimes much more, will reduce the cutthroat population by 90 percent. Nobody yet knows how Yellowstone's bears will adjust to this loss.

Photographers congregate along the Brooks River in Katmai National Park
where grizzlies are easily captured on film.

Outlaws and Livestock

Ranchers as a group have long disliked bears—both black and grizzly—because the bears may prey on their sluggish dull-witted livestock, especially sheep. Who can blame the bears? Sheep are easy pickings—a candy species. A grizzly can acquire a taste for sheep by traveling with a sheep-killing mother. It can also pick up the habit by eating dead sheep left behind by careless or lazy herders who fail to bury them. Once the bear develops a taste for sheep from eating carrion, it can easily move on to harvesting its own mutton. Sometimes the bear kills far more of these docile animals than it can eat.

Some stock-killing grizzlies have gained sufficient local fame to be assigned their own names, often originating with tracks left by feet mutilated in traps. Among them have been Old Club Foot, Old Three Toes, Two Toes, Bloody Paws and Big Foot Mary.

Biologists as well as ranchers have come to expect sheep losses wherever sheep and bears share the range. In Gallatin National Forest, adjacent to Yellowstone National Park in Montana, researchers investigated six allotments where a total of 15,707 sheep grazed and found that bears took one-half of one percent of the sheep over a two-year period. If you are the rancher, this loss becomes significant.

The answer seems simple enough—the only way to save sheep from grizzlies, and bears from avenging ranchers, is to keep sheep off public lands in grizzly bear country. Following the bear's classification as a threatened animal in the lower 48 states under the Endangered Species Act, the U.S. Forest Service revoked grazing permits where grizzlies inhabit the national forests.

Transplanting Bears

If livestock corrupts bears, garbage corrupts them absolutely. In either case the bear that learns to eat "people foods" rarely reforms, and biologists have often tried to solve the problem by moving troublesome bears off to distant wilderness homes. But bears have good memories and a remarkable homing ability. Biologists captured one bear that became a nuisance around a dump in West Yellowstone, Montana, and moved him 90 miles. Eventually the bear was back on the same dump. Two other grizzlies captured at Gardiner at the north entrance of

A grizzly using a footbridge to cross the Brooks River
quickly clears it of human pedestrians.

Yellowstone National Park and moved 50 miles away were back a week later. Another grizzly moved 70 miles was back home in three days.

We have yet to learn how it is that bears navigate and find their way over long distances through strange country. But this ability to find their old homes involves more than simply wandering around at random until coming into familiar territory. Bears have even found their way home over water. In Alaska an immature grizzly was loaded aboard a boat, hauled fifty-eight miles and released on an island in Prince William Sound. He was back in twenty-eight days and his shortest possible route involved swimming through more than six miles of strong tidal currents.

Transplanting trouble-causing grizzlies is a drastic move—costly as well as hazardous to the bear. The hungry bear in strange territory that wanders into a ranch or hunting camp may be shot or trapped. Between 1975 and 1991 the Montana Department of Fish, Wildlife and Parks moved 103 grizzlies at a cost of about a thousand dollars each for offenses ranging from threatening people to garbage dump feeding and depredations on livestock, apiaries and buildings. Within two years, more than one-third of the transplanted bears were dead.

One bear's troubles began one night when he discovered a shabby little cabin near Giefer Creek. Garbage was scattered around and the door stood open. The bear had found a source of easily obtained foods. He quickly became a specialist in robbing cabins and soon racked up an amazing record of destruction. His reputation grew and he soon became known locally as public enemy number one.

State wildlife workers, responding to a series of calls from desperate property owners, finally captured the Giefer Grizzly with a baited snare, drugged him, put a tag in his ear and hauled him off to the wilderness some fifty miles away. They heard no more from the big bear that year and hoped they had solved their problem. But the following spring the renegade was back breaking into cabins again. He was elusive and intelligent, sometimes stealing the bait from sophisticated traps set for him, then moving on to another cabin. Wildlife officers eventually captured him again and moved him north, this time almost to the U.S.–Canada border. He was eventually killed in Canada by a big game hunter.

A grizzly investigates an abandoned boat.
Next pages: The wilderness grizzly makes an annual pilgrimage to spawning streams as the salmon arrive.

Chapter Six

F A M I L Y
L I F E

The annual season of mating is a brief interlude in the adult grizzly's summer. By the time he leaves his winter den the male bear is already producing sperm. By late May his overwhelming drive is to travel and sample the winds for hints of females in estrus.

Mating

The male and female that form a pair bond may associate only briefly, or perhaps travel together for a few days to as long as three weeks. During this time, which peaks about the first two weeks of June, they copulate repeatedly. This is apparently necessary to stimulate the female and induce ovulation. Copulation, during which the male mounts the female from the rear and clasps her with his front legs ordinarily lasts fifteen to twenty minutes. In Yellowstone, researchers clocked one such union that lasted an hour.

Young cubs respond to their mother's indications of warning.

Next pages: A larger cub may serve as lookout while its mother feeds.

Grizzly bears are polygamous. Both males and females may have multiple mates during the breeding season. Females have been known to accept two or three males in the same day. At Montana State University, research biologist Lance Craighead verified that grizzly cubs born in the same litter may have different fathers. Craighead's field research extended over six years in the Arctic National Wildlife Refuge in northeastern Alaska. Using DNA analysis and blood or tissue samples from 153 grizzly bears, Craighead could fit these bears into related bloodlines.

For the grizzly, repeated copulation stimulates ovulation.

Although male grizzlies may begin breeding by the time they are about five years old, males in the Arctic that were successful at fathering young were all at least nine years old. The successful breeders included about half of the adult males. The most successful breeders were not necessarily the largest, boldest males, Craighead found. One of the most successful was the oldest bear he had ever encountered. Biologists determine the age of a bear by extracting a non-functional first premolar tooth from the drugged animal and counting the annual rings in a cross-section of it under a microscope. He was thirty-two years old the last time they saw him.

Female grizzlies do not give birth to their first young until they are five-and-a-half years old, and often not for another two or three years after that. Intervals between litters range from three to five years. Available food helps determine reproductive success; the better-fed female breeds earlier, has bigger litters and raises more young in her lifetime. In Yellowstone, female grizzlies average one litter of 1.9 young every third year.

Females do not normally come into estrus as long as they are lactating. Furthermore, females with cubs may continue to produce milk until their cubs are in their second year. This, plus the fact that there are usually only two cubs, helps account for the bear's slow reproductive rate.

As the mating season winds down males and females quickly revert to their solitary travels, wandering away from each other and slipping easily back into their more normal lifestyle as loners.

Birth

The union of male and female does not guarantee the birth of new cubs. In nature, the mother's survival is always of prime importance and the system that has evolved with the bears is a remarkable example. Even though the egg is fertilized and the embryo begins to grow, its future is uncertain. After it divides to about 200 cells and is scarcely visible to the human eye, it stops growing. At this stage it is known as a blastocyst. For the next five or six months, the system is on hold while the blastocysts simply float free in the uterus waiting for a signal. If the season is one of poor food production, perhaps a disastrous failure of berry crops or the whitebark pine nut crop, and

Next pages: A female grizzly guarding her cubs prepares to meet an approaching male in battle.

the female's store of fat is low for the approaching winter, she aborts and is spared a dangerous drain on her limited winter supply of fat. But, about the time she enters her den for the winter, if she has fed well enough during the summer and fall to support both her body and her new cubs, the blastocysts implant in the wall of her uterus and their growth resumes.

Gestation is brief. The cubs are born in the den in mid-winter toward the end of January, after a scant two months or so of development. They are thinly furred and helpless, and for the next five weeks they are blind. The newborn miniature cubs born of a 300-pound mother and 500-pound father come into the world weighing less than a pound each. Only delayed implantation kept them from weighing ten pounds or so at birth and putting demands on the female's system that she could not survive.

For the rest of the winter the little bears snuggle into their mother's thick fur and live entirely on her rich milk which is high in fat, protein and minerals. By the time plants are greening up with new spring growth and the little grizzlies come out of the den into the daylight for the first time, they will weigh about 15 pounds each.

Not all mothers are equally adept at parenting or equally protective of their young. Most, however, are strict disciplinarians and this has survival value for the youngsters. If the mother indicates to her cubs to "get up that tree," they had best do so without delay because corporal punishment is the norm in the bear family, and to hesitate is to risk a sound swat. This training can save cubs' lives, especially where there are male bears around because the males—which will kill the cubs if they reach them—can't climb trees.

If the mother dies, her inexperienced young cubs will probably die too; but occasionally a cub has shown remarkable ability to survive on its own. One seven-month-old Alaska grizzly cub, orphaned when a hunter shot the mother, was captured and released in the wilderness far from people. It was killed illegally a year later. It had denned, presumably alone, through one winter and until shot was surviving on its own. This may have been an exceptional bear, lucky enough to avoid larger bears and survive without the mother's additional training and protection. Two grizzly cubs orphaned in Glacier National Park are known to have denned on their own, and at least one of them was seen the following summer.

Adoptions

Sometimes a female will adopt another female's cubs. On a July day in 1961, biologist Albert W. Erickson, studying the behavior of grizzlies on Alaska's McNeil River, watched two mother bears, each with three small cubs, come to the water. The females both entered the stream and while they fished for salmon, their cubs socialized. The little cubs soon became so inter-mixed that they looked like one litter and the first female to leave the river was followed by all six cubs.

The female that lost her cubs went about searching and sniffing the air in vain. She then put her nose to the ground and trailed the parade of bears until she caught up. She promptly attacked the other female, but the battle ended abruptly when one of the cubs tumbled into the swift water and was washed downstream. Both mothers splashed in to rescue the swamped cub as it bobbed along on the

A mother bear sends her young cubs into hiding
at the first hint of danger.

current. The mother who had lost her family nudged the swamped youngster ashore on the far side of the river. Together, they wandered off into the bush while the other female departed with her newly formed family of five cubs.

The female with her solitary cub returned shortly and again set off trailing her lost ones. Nobody knows if she eventually reassembled her family. But over the next ten days, whenever the adoptive mother was seen, she still had five cubs with her. The following year the biologists watched for the familiar female and her single young but never saw them again.

Biologists have successfully slipped orphaned cubs into litters of nursing females. This trick works best when the females are still in their winter dens. If tried later in the year the female has to be drugged and have her nostrils rubbed with medicinal salve to mask the odors so she can't sort out the strange cubs by smell and kill them.

Although adult grizzlies are loners, recently weaned young
may continue to travel together.

Leaving Home

The young bears reach a new critical point in their lives when their mothers finally send them out into the world. Of some two hundred litters studied in Yellowstone, about half of the female grizzlies weaned their young at the age of one-and-a-half years while the rest kept their cubs through another winter. If the cubs are too reluctant to leave, their mother may turn on them, chase them, and sometimes attack until the cubs accept the fact that they must go it on their own. Females may wean their young and breed again the same season.

Whether for companionship or security, orphaned and newly weaned littermates may stay together and even den together until mature. They will sometimes defend each other against a common enemy.

Enos Mills once watched three large orphaned cubs over several weeks as they roamed the Sawtooth Mountains of Idaho. One day two hunters shot one of the large cubs and although it was not seriously hurt, its two siblings rushed out of the bushes and attacked the men. One surprised hunter dropped his gun, leaped for the low branches of a nearby tree and was about to climb out of grizzly bear reach when the nearest bear stood up, grabbed him and managed to strip off one of his leggings.

Meanwhile the third cub attacked the second hunter. With a swipe of its paw, the bear rolled the man headlong into the willows, then leaped upon him, cracked two ribs and bit deeply into his shoulder and thigh. The three youngsters then vanished into the brush.

But this was not to be the last seen of the trio. When one of them caught two toes in a bear trap, the other two stayed nearby, standing guard, until the following day when the trapper returned. The trapper's horse panicked, threw the rider off and raced for home with an empty saddle while the pair of enraged young grizzlies chased the unseated trapper up a tree. Meanwhile, the third cub pulled free of its trap by sacrificing two toes, and once more the three young grizzlies escaped into the forest.

According to Mills, the three cubs roamed across forty miles of mountainous terrain until, as young adults, they separated and went their individual ways.

Chapter Seven

INTO
WINTER

A s summer winds down and chill winds sweep over the wilderness, both the grizzly's body and its daily behavior undergo remarkable changes. With the end of the growing season the bear must be ready to sleep the winter away. Weeks of heavy eating, probably day and night, adding up to two pounds a day of body fat, have prepared it for the coming months when natural foods are not available to support its large body and keep it alive. All winter long the bear's fat will be its only source of energy.

In zoos, where animals face no food shortage, bears stay awake in winter. But out on their natural range they meet the bleak winter months by becoming one of nature's most efficient hibernators.

A grizzly becomes aggressive when its space is invaded.

Den

There is evidence that the bear senses instinctively, even when weather is still balmy, that it must prepare a safe place for winter. But denning behavior can vary from bear to bear. Some begin in midsummer to excavate a winter den while others may end up digging with snow swirling around them.

When time comes to start preparing the den, the bear typically ambles off toward some distant mountainside probably remembered from previous years. This is likely to be at an elevation of 8,000 to 10,000 feet, often near the tree line and far from human activity. Where there are forests, the bear will commonly dig its den under a large tree and the roots provide added support for the roof. In the high altitude there is less chance of rainfall and this, plus the fact that the soil is more likely to remain frozen, reduces the chances of a cave-in.

The bear chews off roots that are in the way and uses those long front claws to remove soil and loosen rocks as it excavates its winter home. It may abandon a den in progress and start a new one nearby, and there may be two or three of these "false dens" which are usually smaller than the one finally completed and occupied.

The winter den's size and shape varies from bear to bear and will be matched to the animal's body size. A close fit conserves body heat. Females with young need room for the family to curl up side by side. The occupied den is usually equipped with a mattress of spruce boughs and bear grass or other available vegetation, and pregnant females often top the bed off with a layer of soft grass or moss. This also helps conserve heat.

In some instances, the entrance opens right into the sleeping chamber, but more likely there will be a tunnel sloping slightly uphill to the bed chamber. The tunnel may be five feet long or more and this helps keep the bed dry and warm.

A few fortunate and careful observers have managed to study the grizzly at work on its winter den. One October day, far up on the side of a mountain in Denali National Park, Adolph Murie watched from a distance as a grizzly prepared its winter home. This bear may have been in a hurry. It was late in the season. Eventually, the bear disappeared in the hole but would occasionally back out of the den shoving the dirt away so that it rolled down the hill.

The following summer Murie climbed back up the 45-degree slope to check this den. The top had caved in but he was still able to make a set of measurements. The bed chamber was four feet from the entrance and about five feet in diameter. The tunnel leading to it sloped upward at a 10-degree angle. He later discovered another grizzly's den with a tunnel twelve feet long and this one had been started in mid-summer. It had still not caved in when he paid it a return visited six years later. Grizzlies rarely use the same den more than one year.

Hibernation Trigger

Once the bear accumulates enough fat to see it through the winter its hectic pace gradually winds down. For a while it may wander around sluggishly in the vicinity of the den in a state of lethargy that has been called "walking hibernation." The bear is ready for that long winter sleep. It waits only for the final signal.

The message to hibernate typically comes for Yellowstone bears on a November night with the season's first heavy snowstorm. The bears apparently get advance warning that the storm is coming, perhaps by a change in atmospheric pressure, and begin moving toward the den site several hours ahead of the storm. Across the mountains, grizzlies seem to get the message about the same time, and on this night there is a general movement toward the waiting dens. Soon snow covers the fresh bear tracks leading to the den, hides the entrance and seals the bear in for the winter.

Alaska Department of Fish and Game biologists, however, studying the big brown bears of Kodiak Island, found that these bears, unlike their Yellowstone cousins, did not time their denning to the arrival of the season's first heavy snow nor did they all go to their dens uniformly. In parts of Kodiak Island, where winters are milder, some grizzlies may not even dig a den but instead spend the winter bedded down on the ground in thick brushy areas. During one winter in which the denning bears on the southwestern part of the island were studied, some 25 percent of those wearing radio collars slept outside in the open. From time to time they would stir from their beds briefly and move around in a state of "walking hibernation."

Next pages: With an ample layer of fat, this grizzly is well-prepared for winter hibernation.

Body Changes

The hibernating grizzly is a bear-in-waiting, simply lying there, surviving between summers. Although scientists consider the winter sleep of bears to be true hibernation, their winter condition is different from that of smaller hibernators. The bear is a lighter sleeper. In winter, as the bear goes into hibernation, its heart beat slows from its summertime rate of forty to fifty per minute at rest to eight to twelve beats per minute. But body temperature falls only slightly and this permits the bear to awaken if disturbed. It also permits the bear's body to maintain a metabolic rate near normal, and this is vital to pregnant females that must nourish developing embryos then, beginning in mid-winter, produce milk for their newborn cubs. A bear disturbed in winter may abandon its den, risking a dangerous overdrawal from its limited stores of body fat.

During its long winter sleep the bear will not eat, drink, urinate or defecate. But its body continues to produce urea which would normally be eliminated by urination. If allowed to accumulate, uremia, coupled with dehydration, would kill the bear as surely as it would one of us. But the bear's body recycles the urine. Instead of staying in the bladder the urine is absorbed back into the blood then converted to amino acids which form proteins that help nourish the body.

Meanwhile the bear is losing water as it exhales, but here too it has evolved with a remarkable system for replacing the lost water and avoiding dangerous dehydration. The burning of fat produces water about equal in weight to the fat used. These traits allow the bear to maximize the benefits from its store of fat, put its body functions on hold and slumber through the long winter.

During the winter months the bear continues to lose weight steadily, sometimes as much as two pounds a day, and emerges from its den in spring trimmed down again to an amazing 30 to 50 percent less than it weighed at the beginning of winter.

The Cycle Continues

As long as it lives, this is the order of the grizzly bear's year—from skinny to fat to skinny again. This system, periodically leaving the animal fat and sluggish, would be disastrous for smaller animals that

must constantly elude predators.

The spring awakening comes in late March or early April. But the female and her new cubs may hang around the den for another week or more, and spring storms may still send them back inside. By autumn when their mother leads them into another den where they will spend their first birthday the grizzly cubs normally weigh from 125 to 150 pounds each.

During its second year a cub's weight should climb to 200 to 250 pounds. Now, death by humans becomes the greatest hazard to the young bear's survival. But if it avoids the many hazards associated with people, the young grizzly has a good chance of making it into the adult population.

A bear emerging in spring may have lost up to half its weight during hibernation.

Chapter Eight

WHY BEARS ATTACK PEOPLE

One summer day some years ago in Glacier National Park, a thirty-year-old school teacher had what he thought at first was a stroke of good fortune. He was hiking in the park, now and then pausing to expose more of the film in his movie camera, when he spotted an adult grizzly bear and her furry little cub.

The bears were 150 yards away when the camera began running. Given the bear's speed, this distance could not provide much of a safety margin, but the bear ignored the photographer until he moved to within fifty yards of her. The photographer, glancing again at the tree he would climb if need be, inched closer, and still the bear ignored him.

Then suddenly, he had crossed an invisible line and violated her space. Rangers later speculated that he had worked his way between the female and her cub. She lifted her head and looked right at him.

Bluff charges quickly discourage smaller bears.

Her feeding abandoned, she rushed the photographer at full speed sending him scrambling for his chosen tree.

Getting well up a tree is a good idea if the bear moves toward you, but it is important to choose a nearby tree because a grizzly, traveling 35 miles an hour, can run about twice as fast as the best human sprinter. Running from a predator triggers an attack. The predator is conditioned by experience, or perhaps genetics, to chase down prey trying to escape. Furthermore, the bear can reach farther up a tree than most people realize. The photographer was still trying to gain altitude when he felt the bear's jaws lock onto his foot.

Bears may challenge each other with a deafening roar.

The next thing he knew he was on the ground being rolled around, bitten and slobbered over by an enraged mother grizzly. As bear and man rolled down the steep slope, the photographer reached out and secured a grip on a tree. The bear, unable to stop, kept rolling downhill.

Bears, with their powerful hind legs, are remarkably fast uphill runners, and this female raced back up the slope to finish what she had started. Again, the photographer was ascending the tree when the bear grabbed him. This time he kicked her in the face and he was fortunate—the bear turned and departed.

Later, recovering in the hospital from severe punctures and lacerations on his arms and legs, the hiker urged Park Service people not to harm the bear. "I invaded her space," he said. And so he had.

Keep Your Distance

He had broken perhaps the most important safety guideline for anyone who sees a grizzly—he tried to get closer. A more experienced or cautious grizzly bear observer might have slipped away quietly before being detected by the bear.

We sometimes harbor unreasonable fears of the grizzly bear. The bear pictures gracing the covers of outdoor magazines have nurtured our misconceptions. These outraged beasts stand tall on their hind feet, slobbering and glaring, fangs gleaming, claws long and razor-edged, eager to chew and slash their victims to death.

By standing up, many a bear has given people an excuse to shoot it and claim, "It threatened my life." But the bear standing up on two feet is really trying to get a better look at the scene or pick up clues from the wind. If it attacks it will get down on all four feet to rush its victim, not waddle forward on its hind feet.

Often the bear will stop short and back off, then turn and charge again, maybe coming a little closer with each false charge. Waving the arms and talking to the bear or yelling at it has caused many a bear to give up and leave. One person was carrying a small umbrella which, at the last moment, he popped open in the bear's face causing it to turn and run away. Another, experienced in judo, is said to have given the bear a powerful kick in the throat at the last moment and discouraged the attacker.

But most people are in no position to pull such last minute tricks out of the bag. The best protection against grizzly bears is distance.

Nearly all daytime attacks on people can be traced to the bear's sudden decision that a person has come too close. This reaction to space being invaded can stem from the grizzly's impulse to protect its young or a food source. The bear may also attack if it is surprised by a person suddenly appearing nearby, as sometimes happens when hikers are moving against the wind or through brushy areas where bears are resting in day beds or gathering berries.

One of these berry-picking bears was seriously pursuing his business one day in Denali National Park when Dick Russell came upon him so suddenly that both Russell and the bear were totally surprised. Russell, a wildlife biologist with the Canadian Wildlife Service, described his close call for a group of bear biologists. His account gives a revealing look into bear behavior.

"I walked over a little hump in the ground," said Russell, "and he had his head in a berry patch and discovered me. We just froze in mid-step and looked at each other. Then he turned and walked, didn't run, he walked very methodically in my direction and he came within eight feet of me, facing me with his mouth open and occasionally chopping his teeth. Since there were no trees to climb, I decided the best thing to do was to stand my ground. We always stood our ground and in every instance it worked to turn the bear.

"I had found a dead Dall sheep ram up on top of a mountain that day and was on my way back to camp and I had carried the two horns with me. When the bear approached I started yelling at him and waving one of the horns over my head, I don't know why I did it, but I guess I figured I'd clout him over the nose if he made an actual grab for me. When he got within eight feet he stopped and I continued to yell and wave my arm at him.

"Then he turned sideways with his head lowered and made a very peculiar slavering noise, and then started to retreat, stepping sideways, always with the head down, sort of looking at me out of the corner of one eye. He retreated in this manner to about thirty feet and then turned and walked away.

"But periodically he would suddenly turn 180 degrees and face me and then chop his jaws and sometimes paw the ground and flick his wrist. I think it took him about twenty minutes to retreat three hundred yards. As he approached three hundred yards I could

A bear disturbed in a berry patch may become a serious threat.

BEAR

FREQUENTING AREA

REMOVAL OF THIS SIGN MAY RESULT IN INJURY TO OTHERS and is punishable by fine up to $500 or imprisonment for 6 months or both

tell that he was having difficulty seeing me. He would peer in my direction and move his head around a lot. Finally he turned and started to run away. He ran right across the valley and over the range of mountains on the other side. Needless to say, once he started to run, I collapsed."

But there is no general rule that guarantees safety in the presence of a grizzly. Who can say that a crotchety bear with a toothache won't attack for no apparent reason? In 1983, around Yellowstone National Park, Grizzly Bear No. 15 was a well known bear. Scientists had studied the twelve-year-old grizzly through most of his life. The animal was docile for a grizzly and had never threatened people.

But, on a June night, without warning, No. 15 killed a sleeping camper. Bears that pose the greatest threat to human safety are those conditioned to the human presence, and all his life No. 15

Signs in national parks warn tourists that they are first and foremost in bear country.

had been a garbage eater. He had become habituated to people, and was therefore a greater threat than wilderness bears that are unaccustomed to people.

Obey the Rangers

Perhaps the wonder is that there are not more people injured by grizzly bears. Yellowstone National Park alone attracts more than three million people every year, and rangers here issue some 45,000 permits for people to camp in the backcountry while thousands more take day hikes.

One fact that always impresses me is that the people who seem least likely to be injured by a wild grizzly bear are those who know them best, the professional bear biologists. Serious injuries of biologists by bears, even though they spend hundreds of hours studying grizzlies, are rare. During their eleven-year-long research project in Yellowstone National Park the Craighead research team handled 524 grizzly bears, tracked them day and night for 29,000 hours and made more than 13,000 observations of grizzlies all without a single human injury by a bear. On the other hand, most people attacked by grizzlies have never before seen more than a few, if any, wild bears. Traveling the national parks I've often observed that the park rangers have a greater reluctance than the tourists to get close to wild animals whether elk, moose, bison, or bear. The ranger keeps his or her distance, yielding gracefully to the animal, while the tourist gets up close for the sake of a picture.

To See a Grizzly

In days gone by, a far larger percentage of Yellowstone visitors saw grizzlies than they do now because the park administrators went out of their way to bring the bears and people together. By showing visitors what they most wanted to see, the park management built congressional support for more funds for the park.

Every evening there were bear shows where campers and people from the lodges, sometimes by the hundreds, assembled out back around the dumps to watch bears come in and eat garbage. Benches

Next pages: A pair of Yellowstone grizzlies brings traffic to a halt.

were built around the bear feeding areas.

Rangers sorted out bacon scraps and other choice edibles to make the event more attractive to the bears. A 1926 Park Service guidebook on Yellowstone spoke of some fifty bears hanging around hotels and campgrounds. The guidebook called the park bears "peaceable" and said that they would not "harm you if you let them alone."

This mix of enchanted visitors and "peaceable" grizzlies could not last, and predictably it would be the bears that suffered the consequences. Park attendance grew and rangers became increasingly uneasy about the potential for injury by the bears. These bear sideshows finally ended in 1941, and trucks began hauling the garbage off into the nearby hills away from people.

This bear's body language indicates that it is
prepared to meet a challenge.

In the days of the staged bear shows there was apparently little concern about whether the garbage-fed bears were losing their wildness. The park's wildlife was managed with a heavy hand. Early park supervisors so favored herbivores over predators that their crews of hunters and trappers methodically killed wolves, coyotes and cougars to protect elk, deer and bison. According to Yellowstone Park historian Paul Schullery this manipulation of the park wildlife accounted for the deaths of at least 121 cougars, 132 wolves and more than 4,000 coyotes. The predator killing campaign continued until 1935.

In time, attitudes would change. We came to understand that a national park is not a zoo but is instead a natural area where grizzly and raven, butterfly and wildflower are all elements of a complex community which can be pauperized by loss of its parts.

As Yellowstone attendance grew from 25,000 a year in 1914 to a million in 1948, then doubled and still continued to grow, the chances of people being mauled and perhaps killed by bears increased. The aim today is to keep bears and people at safe distances from each other.

Where bears and people are allowed to associate the bears suffer the greatest losses. During the summer following closure of the bear garbage eating shows, rangers had shot twenty-eight grizzlies for injuring or threatening people. For several years afterward more grizzlies with latent memories of daily garbage banquets died when they came into populated areas. The killing continued. In thirteen years beginning in 1950, rangers had to kill another fifty-one of the bears. In 1968, amid much controversy, the Park Service administered its cure cold turkey and began precipitously closing the garbage dumps. With the dumps closed, the bears began showing up more frequently in park campgrounds where, over the next five years, dangerously high numbers of them were eliminated by park rangers.

Today, with the bears discouraged around the centers of human concentration, only a small percent of Yellowstone visitors ever see a grizzly bear. But the possibility is still a prime reason for traveling there.

Even the world-famous geysers can be upstaged by a bear. One summer day in 1984 the usual crowd was assembled to watch Old Faithful's scheduled eruption when suddenly a footloose, two-year-old, 140 pound female grizzly wandered onto the scene. The Park Service might as well have turned Old Faithful off. Delighted tourists from across America as well as several foreign countries immediately gave the bear their undivided attention while rangers rushed to the scene in force to protect both the people and the bear. The bear hung around until trapped and transplanted into the distant wilderness.

But Yellowstone's grizzlies are still seen by growing numbers of serious bear watchers willing to get up early and devote time and patience to the pursuit. The very best times come in May and June when the big bears roam the mountainsides in search of newborn elk calves, in places like Hayden Valley, Lamar Valley, the slopes of Mount Washington or Pelican Valley. People wishing to see bears should find a high elevation spot where you can see across several miles of open country with binoculars or spotting scope. Bundle up, and take your stand before daybreak. Other watchers will be out so go quietly with no loud talking or slamming of car doors. Be prepared to stay a few hours, and sooner or later you may see bears— and now that they have been re-introduced, wolves as well—especially if you have chosen a spot where elk are abundant. In the face of this age-old drama the elk population continues to prosper.

Avoiding Close Calls

The possibility of a close encounter is always there and this prompts the Park Service to carry out a continual educational program helping visitors understand the nature of the grizzly and how to stay safe in bear country. Still, park rangers are amazed by the attitudes some visitors display toward bears. "We have some years when people see more bears than they do other years," a ranger told me in Yellowstone. When there are food crop failures, the hungry bears range more widely and come more frequently out to the roads and into campgrounds. "This was one of those high-visibility years," the ranger added. "I'm always surprised at how close people might get to a grizzly bear along a park road. Eight feet. Six feet. One person was six feet below a grizzly on a bank. You hear them say things like, 'Isn't it cute? This is neat', and they don't realize that the bear at that moment is making a decision on whether or not to attack."

The first rule to remember in grizzly country is that there are no hard and fast rules that will protect you under all circumstances. But there are precautions that experienced travelers always observe in these national parks and surrounding lands.

Here are some of the rules outlined by rangers of the National Park Service, U.S. Forest Service and state conservation agencies:
- Do not hike at night.
- Do not hike alone. Hike in groups of four or more because bear attacks almost always occur when the bear encounters only one or two people.
- Avoid dense brushy areas where a bear could be bedded.
- If you find fresh bear sign—tracks, scats, scratchings—leave the area immediately.
- Where visibility is limited by weather or the nature of the land-scape, make noise to warn the bear that you are in the vicinity. Bears sometimes react violently when taken by surprise. Wearing bear bells, carrying a rattle made of stones in a can, or singing and talking on the trail may give the bear time to slip away. This is especially impor-tant when hiking into the wind where odors won't warn the bear of your presence.

Campers need to take extra safety precautions to avoid confrontation with a curious—or hungry—grizzly bear.

Next pages: Bears and humans uneasily share prime fishing grounds in Alaska.

- If you see a bear in the distance, detour around it staying upwind.
- Choose a nearby tree to climb if the bear comes toward you, and when you climb go higher than you think you need to
- Discarding a garment or pack may slow the bear down if it stops to investigate.
- Don't run from the bear if there is no place nearby to take refuge. Instead, if the bear charges, and there is no tree for a refuge stay where you are, yell or talk to the bear and wave your arms. Make yourself taller if you can by standing up on a rock or log.
- As a last resort, get on the ground and into the fetal or "cannon-ball" position, protecting head and belly, and play dead—then stay "dead" for some time even after you're sure the bear has gone.
- If close to a bear avoid direct eye contact.
- Do not take a dog into bear country. The dog chased by a bear will likely come running back to you—bear and all.
- Menstruation, sexual activity, and carelessness with human wastes may attract bears.
- Camp away from trails that bears might travel. Remember the bear's superb olfactory sense.
- Strong odors of any kind may bring bears into camp. Carry foods that do not have high odors. Select a cooking and food storage area a considerable distance downhill from your sleeping area, and hang food in plastic bags in trees well above the bear's reach. Secure garbage in plastic bags, keep it out of reach of bears and pack it out with you. Never bury garbage in wilderness areas. Bears and other animals will dig it up.
- Travel and sleep in clean clothes free of food odors. Keep your sleeping bag clean and do not use deodorants or perfumes.
- Carry a can of capsaicin, a spray extracted from cayenne pepper that is a powerful irritant to eyes, nose and throat. Sprayed into the face of an attacking bear, it may discourage the attack.

Encounters between grizzlies and people are dangerous for the bears as well as people. Fear of bears, and sometimes plain opportunism, has prompted the shooting of many bears that didn't need to die.

Our fear of bears keeps many people out of the wild places. While some of us may view this as an important public service rendered by the grizzly, there is a middle ground. Few hikers ever see a grizzly, even at a distance, and if they do, and go by the rules, the experience should leave not scars, but cherished memories.

The teeth of a grizzly are formidable weapons.

Next pages: A lone bear follows a heavily used trail.

Chapter Nine

WHAT THE
FUTURE HOLDS

Threats to the grizzly bear's future grow as more people invade its last wild homesteads. The grizzlies of the lower 48 states, and even in parts of Canada and Alaska, fight for survival against the same forces that have already killed them off in state after state.

But there is a bright spot in the story of America's grizzly bears, and it lies in the fact that human attitudes toward the grizzly have undergone remarkable changes. Where once nearly everyone seemed either unconcerned about their fate or determined to help kill them off, today public opinion is strongly slanted in favor of the grizzlies.

Grizzly cubs stay close by their mother's side their first year of life.
Next pages: Dominant bears command the choice
fishing spots on spawning streams.

In western mountain country the grizzly is one subject sure to pack the hall for a public meeting. This high level of public interest is also reflected in the hunger for books and movies about the life of this mighty bear. A survey in Montana's ranching country in the Mission Mountains, where the big bears are still prominent members of the wild community, found that 61 percent of the residents said they liked having the grizzlies there. Organizations of conservationists, both national and regional, speak in defense of the bears.

Looking back a century or so we find only a few conservationists and scientists concerned about the grizzly's future. William H. Wright who went west in 1883 to hunt grizzlies became so intrigued with the bears that he gave up killing them. He was afraid, as he wrote, that the bear was "well on its way toward extinction." After 25 years of tracking the bears he said, "I had studied the grizzly to hunt him. I came to hunt him in order to study him."

Following World War II, professional wildlifers in growing numbers began the difficult task of studying the grizzlies and adding to our understanding of this complex animal. Today there are so many bear biologists that they have their own professional organization, the International Association for Bear Research and Management, with regular conferences and more than four hundred members, many of them concentrating on grizzly bear research.

Citizen groups have organized specifically to champion the grizzly bear's cause. In Missoula, Montana, The Great Bear Foundation, with more than two thousand members, tracks the life and times of bears and the human developments that impact their habitat. The Foundation then publishes its findings in *Bear News*, a newspaper devoted entirely to bears. Other organizations with special interest in grizzlies include the Craighead Wildlife-Wildlands Institute, and the Yellowstone Grizzly Bear Foundation, as well as The Wilderness Society, National Audubon Society and numerous other conservation organizations all serving as guardians of the great bear's welfare.

Government Involvement

In 1973 the congress of the United States, reflecting growing public concern, passed the Endangered Species Act, perhaps the most important piece of wildlife legislation yet written. Under this new law

The grizzly is a complex animal we are just beginning to understand.
Next pages: An eagle waits patiently for some scraps of food.

the U.S. Fish and Wildlife Service began surveying the nation's wildlife and putting together a list of America's wild plants and animals that seemed to be heading for extinction.

Obviously, the grizzly bear was a candidate for this list. The bears were already gone from nearly all of their former range in the lower 48 states and their numbers were still dwindling. In June 1975 these southern grizzlies living in the remaining remnants of their original range were added to the official list as a "threatened" species.

This entitled them to special protection and management under the new law. The law charged the Fish and Wildlife Service with working out plans to help the grizzlies increase their numbers.

The Fish and Wildlife Service then organized the Interagency Grizzly Bear Committee, a Grizzly Bear Recovery Team with knowledgeable members from state and federal agencies, tribal councils and other groups. This team was to explore ways to rescue the grizzly and try to nurse its numbers back to a safer level.

Biologists identified six areas, or ecosystems, in the lower 48 states where the grizzly still lives or might be brought back. Furthermore, for each ecosystem the recovery team set bear population goals that, if reached, will mark the recovery point for grizzlies in that area. Re-establishing grizzlies in these places, if successful, means saving the wild ecosystems of which the bears are but a part. This will take sizable expenditures of money and, in some cases, probably thirty to forty years of research and management.

Publication of the recovery plan brought more proof of the overwhelming public interest in the beleaguered grizzly. More than five thousand people sent in written comments on the plan. Environmental groups, judging the plan inadequate, especially in protecting grizzly bear habitat, went to court and the recovery plan had to be revised and strengthened.

Meanwhile, federal and state wildlife law enforcement officers assiduously track illegal killing of grizzlies by ranchers, hunters, poachers and others. We no longer let the poachers go with a slap on the wrist. When a Montana poacher killed a grizzly in the Flathead National Forest, another citizen promptly led wildlife officers to the scene. This good deed earned the informer a $5,000 reward and the poacher an $8,500 fine plus two years probation.

The bear's size, shoulder hump and dished face easily identify it as a grizzly.
Next pages: Further measures need to be taken
to ensure the grizzly's survival.

132

No sooner did the grizzlies of the Greater Yellowstone Ecosystem appear to make modest gains in numbers in the early 1990s than there was talk of taking them off the list of threatened species. This would relax the legal barriers that protect grizzly habitat under the Endangered Species Act. Others, however, insisted that the grizzly was by no means safe.

Whether or not the grizzly will still survive south of Canada a century from now, only our descendants will know. But without strong public support for the bear, the loggers, miners, road builders and various developers will surely carve away at the wild lands until the last grizzly bear is homeless.

Grizzlies are notoriously difficult to count. Some biologists believe that Yellowstone grizzlies are increasing, others that the population is stable, and some fear that it is declining or soon will be. Any decline in the population is serious. Says David Mattson, bear researcher with the National Biological Service, "A grizzly decline of only one-half of one percent a year would eventually be terminal."

Charles Jonkel, internationally known authority on bears and Director of the Ursid Research Center in Missoula, Montana, believes that the Yellowstone grizzlies may have reached the carrying capacity of their habitat. And the developers are moving in and chipping away at the bear's world.

Optimists find reasons to believe that the grizzly still has a future, as support for the bear grows and people make their views heard among politicians and public officials. The U.S. Forest Service moved sheep out of national forest grizzly country and closed hundreds of miles of forest roads. Fewer bears are killed by people. And many believe that the grizzly is much better off today that it was in 1975 when it was first listed as a threatened species.

If we can allow space for the bear, there may yet be grizzlies in Yellowstone a hundred years from now. But some observers wonder if all the feisty bears that challenge people will have been methodically weeded out, leaving only docile creatures resembling old-time grizzlies in form but not in spirit.

The mighty grizzly is more than a bear—it is a symbol, a reminder of the time when western mountains were wild and the grizzly ruled. The grizzlies, even if they could adapt after the manner of the coyote, would be out of place among soccer fields and lawn mowers. But if we care enough to leave room for the bears, and protect them from people, they can continue to enrich this world for generations to come.

The need to lay on fat for winter keeps the grizzly busy foraging day and night.

WHERE TO SEE
GRIZZLIES IN ALASKA

For more information on where to see Alaska's grizzlies
contact the following authorities.

Brooks River
    Superintendent
    Katmai National Park
    P.O. Box 7
    King Salmon, AK 99613
    (907)246-3305

McNeil River State Game Sanctuary
    Alaska Department of Fish and Game
    333 Raspberry Road
    Anchorage, AK 99518
    (907)267-2179

Denali National Park
    Superintendent
    Denali National Park
    P.O. Box 9
    McKinley Park, AK 99755
    (907)683-2294

Pack Creek on Admiralty Island
    U.S. Forest Service Information Center
    Centennial Hall
    101 Egan Drive
    Juneau, AK 99801
    (907)586-8751

The best time to see grizzlies is during spawning,
when their attentions are otherwise occupied.
Next pages: A grizzly pauses midstream to consume a freshly caught salmon.

FURTHER READING

Bauer, Erwin A. 1985. *Bear in Their World*. Outdoor Life Books. New York.

Craighead, Frank C. Jr., 1979. *Track of the Grizzly*. Sierra Club Books. San Francisco.

Herrero, Stephen. 1985. *Bear Attacks*. Nick Lyons Books. New York.

McCracken, Harold. 1955. *The Beast that Walks Like a Man*. Hanover House. New York.

Murie, Adolph. 1961. *A Naturalist In Alaska*. Devin-Adair Co. New York.

1944. *The Wolves of Mount McKinley*. U.S. Fish and Wildlife Service. Washington, D.C.

Schneider, Bill. 1977. *Where the Grizzly Walks*. Mountain Press Publishing Co. Missoula, Montana.

Schullery, Paul. 1980. *The Bears of Yellowstone*. Yellowstone Library and Museum Association, Yellowstone N.P.

Stirling, Ian. 1993. Consulting Editor. Multiple Authors. *Bears: Majestic Creatures of the Wild*. Rodale Press. Emmaus, Pennsylvania.

Storer, Tracy I. and Trevis, Lloyd P. Jr., 1955. *California Grizzly*. University of California Press, Berkeley, and 1978, University of Nebraska Press. Lincoln, Nebraska.

Wright, William H. 1909. *The Grizzly Bear*. Charles Scribner's Sons, and 1977 University of Nebraska Press. Lincoln, Nebraska.

Grizzlies keep the "wild" in wilderness.